Stress

Recess

❖❖❖

The A B Cs

by

Richard DeForest Erickson

Cover by Michael Dear
Printed by Elk River Printing

DEFOREST PRESS
Box 1305 Elk River, MN 55330

STRESS RECESS / THE ABCs

Cover by Michael Dear

Original text and arrangement by Rhea
Beaudry
Revisions by Julie Fish

Consultation by Julie Fish and Bill Fish,
Chief Honchos, Elk River Printing

Preface

An introduction or preface is used for a lot of things. It can serve as a vehicle with which to give rationale for even writing the book. It can be a defense for the direction of the author's thinking. It can be used as a first chapter...sometimes as lengthy...by which to establish the foundation for everything to follow. It can be the "definition" of the subject...in this case, stress and stress management. Or, and very commonly, the preface is the section in the book in which to thank everyone who has contributed, supported, encouraged, inspired, or, in any way, been part of the process of the publication.

I am at a time in my life when I want to say "Thanks" to many people for many things. However, I choose to thank them very personally. Each of those special people, young and old, will be inducted into Erickson's Order of the Silver Rose. I am grateful to be surrounded by many special people. Somehow, I always want to let them know just <u>how</u> special.

I will only list the first two members of
The Order of the Silver Rose:
The Mothers of the Clan......

Elsie Comstock Erickson
Minda Loftus Olson

...With my deepest love and appreciation

In Loving Memory
of
DeForest Prouty Erickson
who, by his quiet simplicity,
taught me the gentle side of life.

Table of Contents

Avoid ⁊ Alter ⁊ Accept

I n dealing with life's conflicts and configurations, most people want easy answers. In my opinion, this little threesome carries the simplest approach to many stressful issues: avoid it, alter it, or accept it. It is intriguing how many of us repeatedly set ourselves up for pain by putting ourselves (there's an ownership in "<u>our-selves</u>") into stressful scenes and situations. I remember the very sensitive lady who grieved dreadfully that her husband had left her after thirty years of marriage. Her children complained that she constantly played and replayed a Country-Western record. These "somebody done somebody wrong" songs were <u>their</u> songs. She would put on the record and weep her way through the series of agonizing lyrics. They had tried hiding, even destroying the record. She'd simply buy another. They detested the music, and hated to see her crying all the time. When the kids (young adults) asked me for help, I suggested a special Christmas present for "openers". After Christmas, she told me how delighted she was with their gift to her, a set of stereo headphones. She was still weeping when they came home, but they didn't have to listen to the music!

If the stressful element is a person, it seems better to understand a basic in life: It's tough (maybe impossible) to change (alter) someone else; it's also wise to work to <u>accept</u> others as they are, even if that means making some <u>adjustment</u> in the relationship and how you see that person. Some people are probably best <u>avoided</u>! Yes, I'm aware that that is <u>not</u> always easy or (with some) even possible. However, at times, we let ourselves become prisoners to relationships. The more passive we are, it seems, the more likely we'll become victims of predatory people who control us with demands and guilt.

Along this line, I've found it helpful to understand that there are only two purposes for human communication: (1) to share information, and (2) to control. For example, isn't it interesting to look at public education with that perspective? Most teachers go into teaching in order to help children, to share information. Yet, what do most school kids complain about?...That they feel controlled. That's a strange misunderstanding in communication. Teachers are usually thrilled, sometimes amazed, when they have kids who <u>want</u> to learn.

When it comes to people who try to control us with guilt, there are some who should be avoided. This, again, is most difficult for the passive, compliant, pleasing of us. Maybe we have to say, "It's not <u>your</u> fault; I'm just too weak to be around someone as strong as you."

Be Yourself...
at Least Once a Day

Sound strange? Not if you're like so many who say, "I don't seem to be who I want to be". Of course, part of that can be due to the fact that we can spend so much energy living out what others want us to be and do. Actually, it may take real effort for some of us to "be ourselves" once in a while, let alone every day. How many of us have difficulty turning off the telephone, because we have to be available? One woman sent me a long letter following a stress management seminar. She thanked me profusely for giving her permission to turn off her phone "even when I'm in the house". With the machinery we have today, it's possible to be available at any time and anywhere. This is an increasing hazard. Many years ago, I had a counseling client who would call at two in the morning, and always open with the same question: "You're not busy, are you?" (In that cloudy hour, I could have engaged her in philosophical interchange over "What's busy?"... "What's time?"...."To whom does time belong?"...especially at 2 a.m.)

You can see that our lives can get exceedingly cluttered if we are always (because of modern electronics and "conveniences") available and always subject to the demands and expectations of others. It seems clearly possible to be lost in all those other "plans" for our time and energies. We humans have at least three ways of viewing ourselves: (1) How others see us, (2) How we <u>think</u> others see us, and (3) How we see ourselves.

While this may be worth a chapter (or a book) in itself, it is worth it for us to try to determine how we choose to view ourselves, individually. For example, I could live most of my life out in reaction to how I <u>think</u> others see me...and be wrong in the first interpretation. I may also live with a perception of myself which is false. (A classic is the slim person who <u>thinks</u> he's fat.) Unfortunately, we draw so much of our self-image from the words that echo out of the past (like cruel judgments) and then live with false perceptions that affect how we function today.

By the way, this is one of many reasons for having a friend or two who can encourage us to be ourselves...just as we are.

The Serenity Prayer
God, grant me the serenity
to accept the things I cannot change,
Courage to change the things I can,
and wisdom to know the difference.
Living one day at a time,
accepting hardship as a pathway
to peace,
Taking, as Jesus did, this sinful world as it is,
not as I would have it.
Trusting that You will make all things right
if I surrender to Your will;
so that I may be reasonably happy
in this life,
and supremely happy with You
in the next.
Amen.

-Reinhold Niebuhr

Control...Commitment...Challenge

Here again, I'd like to use a trinity: Control, Commitment, Challenge. The business world has done much research to see how and why people function well, and what seems to be needed in such functioning in the work place. This threesome comes out of such study, and I think it has valid application in how we deal with the stress of living. Most of us are readily aware of our need for control in our own lives and how upset we can be by the loss of control. Obviously, the major enemy, death, is the great intruder in any life. Death takes over, as does a common forerunner, sickness. As the intruder, it interrupts the flow of life. It intercedes in our plans and expectations. Naturally, in the shadow of sickness and death, we suffer loss of control. But we seem to have a deep need for control in everyday things more minimal and mundane than sickness and death. While control can be another problem issue when taken to extremes... as in those we call "control freaks"...especially and typically in "independent" America, there is a place for normal daily control in our lives. It is like our need to have a "voice in the process" of things.

We also need to have <u>commitment</u> to something, usually something bigger than ourselves and beyond ourselves. It may be the excellent product, the cause or calling in life. (It is along these lines, probably, that many "lose heart" when a marriage is "broken" or even when the children grow up and leave. If all energy is committed to these family elements, it is no wonder that when there's a loss there, that the world seems to crumble and crash.)

A third facet of this triad is <u>challenge.</u> I must admit that I do not always see this as evident in everybody. It may not always be found in some working situations, or even in some private lives. However, for the sake of health and wholeness, I believe challenge is crucial in some form. I knew a man who admitted that he'd worked with the same factory for twenty-six years, and that the work he did never elevated beyond basic tedium. He was bored at work, but tolerated it because it was secure...and assured a retirement. That was his vocation. His avocation, however, was wood carving. Having an interest as a novice carver, I asked to see a couple of pieces of his work. I was amazed at the exquisite beauty and intricate detail in his carvings of wood ducks and mallards. This was where he found his challenge...in his creative outlet...a constant reaching for artistic perfection.

1998 Note:
That carver and his wife have both retired. Now he enjoys his craft, and she enjoys marketing those great pieces of peace.

Dare to be Imperfect

At first look, that may seem strange to some, especially those of us who never have any pretense of <u>being</u> perfect. I, for one, like to quote to my friends an old Ashleigh Brilliant phrase: "I'm here in this world to serve as a warning to others!"

I, personally, believe perfectionism is a curse. At the outset, I should say something to my Christian friends who quote: "Be ye perfect, as your Heavenly Father is perfect." The actual translation of the word used as "perfect" there is more aptly (and honestly) "complete", which is also one of the definitions of "perfect". To them I also say, "Perfectionism is lousy theology." Does that mean that we shouldn't <u>strive</u> for perfection? No...My carving friend created what I called "perfect" ducks. (He always disagreed. He could see the flaws.)

Maybe I can best express it this way:

> Striving for it and
> being <u>driven</u> by it
> are two different things.

How many things (of work and fun) do we put off simply because we're sure it won't be good enough...even before we begin? How I admire those who just dive in and <u>do it</u>, even with something new. I remember how long I put off my first wallpapering venture...having listened to people who said how difficult it was to hang wallpaper. Having all the paper, glue, equipment, I put it off for six months. It would take too long, not be good enough, be too complicated. Finally, when I dove into it, I found that...for me...it was actually fun!

Most of us, of course, learned the curse of being controlled by perfectionism and its crippling effects when we were children. We may have been cautioned, criticized, ridiculed, intimidated...by elders and peers, whether cruel or caring.Here's one great line for parents from a psychologist, Barbara Kuczen:

> "If you would have a perfect child,

remain childless!"

We need to discover...some of us, at least, to take risks in order to break free...It's been called the freedom to fail. Once in a while, on a Saturday morning, I used to say to my young son, "Grab a hammer, Mike...let's go make mistakes!"

> *"Bachelors' wives*
> *and old maids' children*
> *are always perfect."*

> -Chamfort (1741-1794)

Express

Express can be seen as connected to most of the other ABCs in this gathering. Tragically, so much wisdom and greatness is locked up in people who are simply afraid of making mistakes, being considered foolish or stupid, being misunderstood. After many years as a therapist and pastor, I'm convinced that we do not suffer so much from <u>over</u>-expression as from <u>under-</u>expression. For example, it has long been known that one of the greatest common fears people have is speaking in front of groups. Seventy-five percent of people are frightened of this experience...some even terrified by it. (What this usually means is that the minority - 25% - are given the floor!) It also means that most of the wisdom is locked inside the silent majority. In terms of just verbal expression, some of us know that if we don't say what's in our minds, we get headaches!

At the risk of being too philosophical, I see this issue as going beyond just being verbally expressive and external. Let's use what can be another triad: grief, anger, and guilt. These three normal human reactions are not intended to be maintained as constant, chronic forces in the individual person. While normal, if continued over an extended time, each becomes abnormal and destructive to the system. Take a moment for a note on each.

Shakespeare said, "Give words to your grief."

Jesus said. "Never let the sun set on your anger." He also indicated, "If you have offended someone, make amends." To put it another way, "Confess and be reconciled."

Part of the system of expression also fits in the area of creative extension of the self. A good search in life for many of us could be some avenue or media of artistic expression. For some, this will certainly be in music, whether for and with others, or just for "myself" and my own enjoyment. The key here is "enjoyment". (Look up the word.) An important process for my comfort in life and for management of stress may be finding an area or arena in which I <u>enjoy expression.</u> Those who wish to delve into this more deeply might consider the concept of shifting from left brain (analytical/critical) to right brain (creative/free) by doing something different and artistic like playing the piano or painting.

No matter what direction Expression takes, it can help greatly if it is sometimes shared with another element...a friend.

> *"Friendship*
> *improves happiness,*
> *abates misery,*
> *by doubling our joy*
> *and dividing our grief."*
>
> *-Addison (1672-1719)*

Forgive

To some, this may seem more like a sermon topic than a stress issue. Over the years, I've felt it is a major spiritual and psychological problem that goes much deeper than being simply religious. While that may be very obvious to those of us that have a Judeo-Christian background (and most other religious histories), it is intriguing how many seem to have no awareness of the power of "holding grudges and gripes" in one's life.

Maybe one way to approach the idea and importance of "forgiving" is to make a connection with another power triad of emotions: Guilt, Anger, and Grief...(or, to abbreviate, GAG!) These are normal facets of living out all our lives. Again, they are not only issues for the religious. They are "normalcy", at times, for each of us. However, we are not supposed to dwell within the territory of Guilt, Anger or Grief permanently. They all (while normal in reaction to situations in life) carry the potential for pain and destruction. They can all be immobilizing. Briefly, do your own mind-search and note the memories and images of persons trapped in Guilt, blinded by Anger, stuck in Grief.

While, in this series, I could put Guilt, Anger and Grief in other places in the Stress Alphabet, they fit together because they are (if extended) antithetical (I like that word!) to peace and comfort in life. They (GAG) are, in themselves, stressful stressors. Anger is at the very center. With good reason (and even better spirit) Dr. Martin Luther King, Jr. once wrote, "I will never allow anyone to lower me to the level of hate". Jesus, King's inspiration, said, "Never let the sun set on your anger."

Anger is, if maintained, a constrictive element to the system. Oh well, "forgive me for" (here meaning "allow me to") call Anger a "constipant." (No, the word is not in the dictionary, but you know what I mean!) When we hold on to Anger, it goes deeper and becomes other, more permanent stuff. It can become resentment, generalized bitterness; it can become <u>part</u> of us, so that instead of being angry, we become Angry people. It's a "constipant" because it keeps us from being free. Maybe Anger is the "gift that keeps on giving." Another note: Some people say "Forgive and forget", like the words are Biblical and have to go together. "Forget" may be nice, but not necessary and not always humanly possible. Forgiving is an intentional gift that may even re-establish a relationship (once broken). It will probably, at least, help set us free.

Now, shall we call Forgiveness a laxative...(or do I need to ask your forgiveness for that?)

"Two persons cannot be friends
if they cannot forgive each
other's little failings."

-Bruyere (1645-1696)

Gratitude

Most of us grew up being told, "Count your blessings", and "Be thankful". I think most parents try to pass on a sense of gratitude or gratefulness to their children. This is another one of those concepts that is a stress-issue. Dealing with stressors and stress-reactions is not only a matter of what we <u>do</u> in our lives, but it is also important how we <u>see</u> those things that happen around us and to us. For example, some of us spend a goodly amount of our energies worrying about what other people have and do. It used to be called "Keeping up with the Joneses". (I've known a lot of "Joneses" who wondered what all the fuss was about!) In this vein, the <u>Desiderata</u> makes a statement: "Do not compare yourself to others". Meanwhile, many of us admire the person who seems to "march to a different drummer" and take a different path. Maybe when I'm being myself (at least once a day), I can stop and survey <u>my</u> own world and find those elements for which I am simply grateful. Secker said, "He enjoys much who is thankful for little; a grateful mind is both a great and happy mind".

So what does this have to do with stress? Well, for one thing, a moment's thankfulness is, in itself, a Stress Recess. For example, I'm a Sunset nut; I've been known by my family to take a roll of film just shooting sunset shots while on vacation. I really like the TV commercial (though I don't remember the product!) where the father and his little boy watch a sunset together. When the sun goes all the way down, the little boy says, "Do it again, Dad!"

Sometimes our complaining can become a disease called cynicism which contaminates us (and many around us) to the degree that we can actually "see" nothing "good", nothing for which we can be grateful. One of my personal regrets is that I can never thank all those who give me so much in moments of tenderness and joy...and who, many times, don't even know the great gifts they are giving to those around. The smile of the littlest child is a gift. The music from someone's heart is a gift. Patience from family and co-workers is a gift. I'm grateful that my plumber takes care of our old house (and my mistakes) cheaper than I can. I'm grateful that the local florist has roses even in a Minnesota winter. I'm grateful that the drug store has after-shave samplers, so I can freshen up in the middle of the work-day. (But now I'm being "ridiculous"...and I'm grateful that some let me <u>be</u> ridiculous without ridiculing me for it!) In other words, I'm grateful that so many around me are so gracious.

Now, you see, I've had a moment today for my own celebration of this letter "G". As a Stress Recess, I hope it's been as good for you...as it has for me!

Humor

"Laugh and the whole world laughs with you,
  Weep and you weep alone,
For the sad old earth must borrow its mirth,
  But has trouble enough of its own."

-Ella Wheeler Wilcox (1883)

In talking about HUMOR in the world of stress, we find both how we <u>see</u> and how we <u>react</u> to situations. We all have times when we have difficulty seeing or understanding why something is "so funny" to someone else. Some comedians and TV sitcoms are uproarious to others, while they're not funny to me at all. On the other hand, mention Red Skelton, Danny Kaye, or Tim Conway and you'll get a smile from me. Just their names conjure up images and voices that are funny, even joyful, to me. (Actually, mention the names of our grandchildren, and you'll get the same kind of reaction! Remember John Denver's "He Makes Me Giggle?")

Norman Cousins, during his healing process,

used old comic movies to intentionally tickle his funny bone, to stimulate laughter. He used this approach to actually adjust his perception of things, of the world. One of the definitions for "humor" is "one's disposition or state of mind; mood."

It should probably be stated that not all humor is "humorous". I, for one, see little "funny" in sarcasm. Sarcasm is the lowest form of humor, in that it ridicules (makes to look ridiculous") someone else. Sarcasm is calculated to hurt the other person. It is, in itself, "stressful"; it has no place as a "stress recess".

While this may all seem to put too much seriousness into the subject of HUMOR, ask the cartoonists and comedians. For them, it's serious business. I think, for example, an interesting private search would be to ask acquaintances a simple question: "What makes you laugh?" I have some "routines" every day that help me "lighten up" and laugh. (It's not important enough to take space here, but if you ask me, I'll tell you.)

There's a man in our congregation who has a

joke every time we talk. I've come to expect a "smile a day" from him; I've yet to be disappointed. I don't expect that from everyone, but this person is special in that way. It's like his "signature", like the doctor I knew years ago who always wore a fresh-cut flower every day. The smile, the laugh, the humor is so crucial to life and joy in life. In order to live life...and enjoy it anyway, we need to have moments...sometimes intentional...of levity. It also helps to be conscious of those joy-bringers around us...some of the "right to the end". One great man, on his death bed, said to a worried friend, "Die? That's the <u>last</u> thing I'm going to do!!"

Intentionalize

Intention has a sound that rings with direction, goal-setting, making choices. This may be so obvious to some because it seems so clear that we have to make choices, decisions in life. However, I'm always impressed by the number of people I've known who treat life like it's all a matter of "que serah serah, whatever will be will be". Rather than being intentional in living, they live life like it's all an accident (and like <u>they</u> are just accidents...waiting to happen.) Now, you may ask, what's this have to do with stress, and how we handle stressors in life. Again, if we just leave everything "up for grabs", we leave ourselves open to just being controlled by circumstances, sometimes circumstances <u>within</u> our control. "An ounce of prevention is worth a pound of cure", we used to hear; sometimes it looks like we spend only one-sixteenth of our energy on prevention and sixteen times as much on crisis. Using that metaphor, a related stress-issue is that faced by many of our community servants...teachers, social workers, etc. So much energy can be taken up dealing with crisis and resistance, that there's little left for the joy of teaching and helping those who <u>want</u> to learn, who <u>want</u> help. I mention this because there is a major factor of burn-out for community servants here...a factor not always recognized by community members less involved in the "front lines" of contact.

Intentionality involves being directive, proactive, choosing to initiate. Therefore, it involves taking control and responsibility. It means choosing to <u>not</u> just be passive, to <u>not</u> just wait for something to happen, hoping things will "work out". It's actually guaranteed that "things will work out". They just might not "work out" the way we want them to. Some of us don't want to make choices, decisions, because we are afraid of making mistakes. But doing <u>nothing</u> <u>is</u> still a choice. I think I'd rather make a mistake than just be a passive victim to "accidental circumstances" or to someone else's decisiveness. (There may always be someone else around who would like to be able to decide how I should use my energies and resources.)

Intentions, if practiced, can become good habits. Let me give a homey example: I've always felt my wife has the best sales resistance of anyone I know. If anyone (and there are many attempts these days) tries to call our home to sell something and she answers, there will be <u>no</u> sale! Think of the stress-energy that saves, because of the prior intentional choice: no purchases by phone contact. She's gracious on the phone, but FIRM. Oh, you ask, what about the stress on the sales caller? Well, at least it was a <u>nice</u> "no".

Justify Your Interests

ollowing Intentionality, it may be important for some to actually choose to <u>justify</u>
a particular hobby or interest. Again,
some have no problem here, but I'm more con-
cerned about those who let their own healthy
interests get squeezed out by the demands of
other people's interests.) When this happens, we
may not have much left of a life of our own. A
hobby or "pastime" may actually be a great
daily prevention of stress conflicts for many of
us. The definition of "pastime" may actually be
a great daily prevention of stress conflicts for
many of us. The definition of "pastime" is a
good one: "That which amuses or makes time
pass agreeably; diversion; recreation."

Now, it may seem petty and picky to suggest
that I should have to "justify" (make or judge
acceptable) my hobby. However, I've known
many people who have a special pastime that
holds special joy for them (in comfort, peace,
creativity, diversion from work and worry), but

they have dropped the interest and the involvement because they'd become convicted with guilt about the time and/or money spent. (Yes, here we may have a personal...sometimes marital...debate going on!) Even the word "justify" can have guilt-connections, since it may mean doing what one simply wants to do. This is where intentionality hooks in again. We may need to intentionally program our schedules to include that hobby or interest. If we don't set the time and energy aside, other demands will probably smother the interest out. For most of us, this is probably very obvious. We can remember all kinds of situations where some "enjoyment" was pushed aside and squeezed out by other things which seemed more crucial, more important. Here a basic reality of life might be mentioned. We humans are limited by time and space. Or let me offer another maxim: Every action demands an exclusion. We are polyphasic thinkers...we can think about any number of things...and worry about them all...moving from one to another. However, time and space limits us to being able to usually <u>do</u> one thing at a time. (Ever found yourself frozen in place, doing nothing, while worrying your way through a whole landscape of things you <u>should</u> do?) My grandfather used to say,

> *"Worry is like a rocking chair..*
> *It makes a lot of motion,*
> *but doesn't get you anywhere."*

Maybe it's appropriate to go back to the concept of vocation and avocation again. Vocation is what most of us do in "making a living". It may not be what we most <u>enjoy</u> doing. Avocation is closer to what may be the more desired "occupation" of time. Some of us have made an intentional acceptance of this difficult reality. We may also have to intentionally justify some special interest in order to be sure that our lives include some joyful pursuit.

Know Yourself

gain, in the continuation of the alphabet of stress-aids, I'd like to suggest an "umbrella" concept that is crucial if we wish to curb and prevent stress conflict in our lives. "Know thyself" is an age-old dictum from the sage philosophers. To make it simple, let's quote Menander:

> *"'Know thyself' means this,*
> *that you get acquainted with*
> *what you know, and what you can do."*

Let's take that statement for a little walk and see how it might connect to the issue of relieving stress. We encourage children to learn and to grow and to explore in life, so they can expand their horizons and enjoy fruitful, productive lives. We also want them to find out what their talents are. If we have a budding Mozart, we usually nurture and encourage that musical interest and ability. I, for one, can't read music, but I'm a long-time frustrated musician! As a young boy, I gave up free piano lessons to play baseball...Now I can play neither baseball nor the piano. The loss is not to the worlds of sports or music - the loss is mine. At my age, to play baseball would never be important. To play the piano would be a great satisfaction...and a great added stress reliever.

I hope you can read my point woven into this brief narrative: Choices in interests and talents are usually made quite young. Encouragement may make a difference in those choices, but the choices (decisions) set us on the paths we take. (You could play that concept out in many ways. For example, look at the issue of choosing a mate and partner for life. An adage I would encourage to the young: "Know who you are, and where you're going...THEN choose the one you wish to take with you." I know...easier said than done. But if you look at those three steps, we usually do them in reverse.

Past, Present, Future...In some ways, we've been alluding to that triad. One great philosopher said, "The unexamined life is not worth living." That's quite judgmental; but, at the very least, the unexamined life leaves me in a very shadowed world. To go back to a previous chapter, to another triad, there may be three facets in knowing ourselves: how I see myself; how others see me; and how I <u>think</u> others see me. Most of us make adjustments in our lives based on our experiences in the past...in order to affect our present...which also affects our future. We use feedback from the outside world to understand ourselves...and how we affect others. A simple, slightly abrasive example: Years ago, a loveable little boy, age 5, saw me for some counseling. He liked me...enough that he sometimes chose to sit on my lap (like he did with his grandfather). One day, sitting on my lap, he informed me tenderly, "You have bad breath". Note: This was at least fifteen years ago. No one else has ever registered that honest candor with me, before or since. That gentle little boy never pulled away; he didn't stay away; he didn't avoid me. There was something so honest and so candid in his observation that I simply said, "I'm sorry...and thank you for telling me." He said, "That's okay", put his hand on my shoulder and said, "When can we talk again?"

In that moment, the little "Know Thyself" helped the bigger "Know Thyself"...know himself a little better.

"'Know thyself' means this,
    that you get acquainted
    with what you know,
    and what you can do."
                -Menander (342-291 B.C.)

Love

Last chapter we looked at knowing yourself. To make this move to LOVE may seem strange, but it has long seemed to me to be one of the most obvious stressors. If, as the old saying goes, "Love makes the world go 'round", it also bounces and jerks the world (or us) around. What I'm pointing at today is a subject worth a whole book; but I don't have to write it. For those of you who would like to search further, I'll mention two: <u>The Four Loves</u> by C.S. Lewis and <u>The</u> <u>Art of Loving</u> by Erich Fromm.

"What's love got to do with it (stress)?" Most of us have experienced the stress of love in many ways. The ancient Greeks were wiser than we in their use of the word and concepts about love. They designated four great loves: storge (affection), philos (friendship), eros (sensual love), agape (unconditional love...God's love). In stress-concern, I see this as another "umbrella" concept - broad, but very important. In this brief space, let's try to touch it in terms of its greatest impact, in personal relationships. The easiest and gentlest "love" is probably affection. We can feel that for little children and even pets, including someone else's children and pets. It's gentle, tender, soft in its feeling, more like the purring of a kitten. Friendship is deeper, abiding, sharing in its nature, not easily felt with everyone, or even many. It's reserved for the very few...probably especially as we mature and experience friendship's honest demands. Eros is powerful and multiplex. While we believe it should be reserved for maturity, it rarely waits. It involves the sexual-sensual but goes much further and deeper in its own scope. While it may be the greatest source of poetic creativity, it is also the source of much human agony and suffering. (Like the old pop song said, "What do you get when you fall in love?" You get sick to your stomach!) While eros is so important in our lives, it also is the dangerous territory of "fatal attraction" and obsessive, addictive "I can't live without you" love. Now, if you've followed this far, let your mind expand on this image: Ever known of a situation where one was "in love" and the other was "in like"? There's a big difference between "I am in love with you" and "I am in <u>like</u> with you"; however, we haven't always been wise enough to express (or even know) the difference. Where affection and friendship are not usually prone to jealousy...eros is capable of extreme, even rageful jealousy. (Hollywood makes a lot a money on this one...Disney is more likely to make tender use of the first two loves.)

Agape is a concept many of God's children know as "unconditional love". Children (of all ages) need, more than anything else, acceptance. Most parents nurture their own with this kind of love. It is, I believe, the gift that actually takes away thirst...the water of life. But that's another subject...maybe more timeless and spaceless. This book is not spaceless, nor is it unconditional. Happy loving...as stressful as that can be.

Money...Management and Misery

Interesting...the word "misery", commonly used by us to speak of "great unhappiness and emotional distress" comes out of "miser": "a mean, grasping person; one who lives miserably in order to hoard his wealth." At the outset, when I choose to use money for the M in the ABCs of Stress, it is not because I claim to be an expert in the pursuit, use, or management of the stuff. Anyone who knows me, especially those few who have lived with me, would be my immediate "discreditors"! But in "Tax Week", it seems an obvious choice in my list of M's, and it's one that's an obvious stressor for all of us. In marriage, it's one of the three main conflict issues. (You pick the other two.) Money has been called the "root of all evil". (Actually, the Biblical quote is, "The love of money is the root of all evil.") Probably most of the readers are comfortable enough, but we all know that actual poverty is existent in the midst of "plenty"...and in the midst of "greed". While

I do not wish to make this "sermonic", it is possible for most of us to launch into a verbal tirade regarding the use and misuse of the commodity of currency in society. Every day we joke about winning the lottery...or one of us may get to take a three-point shot for one million dollars...strange world of high finance and advertising!

All of this illustrates that we have many different attitudes about money and its use. Many quotes are available. I like Bacon: "Money is like manure...of very little use, except it can be spread."

Again, I will not, in these few lines, try to tell anyone else what to do with money; I only wish to indicate its power as a stress issue. Maybe this is another area where it is important to "know yourself" in relation to money. I remember the man who crumbled at age forty-five. Depressed, broken, suicidal, in spite of a good and happy family and relative comfort in a secure job, he had failed to achieve his long-time goal. Years before, he had made an oath to himself that he would be a millionaire by age forty-five. To be simplistic and brief, he couldn't adjust his own expectations. (I have decided, at this time in my life, I wouldn't know how to manage a million dollars; therefore you can take my place in the Lottery! This is not an important issue...just an attitude.)

In relationships, like marriage, conflicts will arise because of different values and attitudes about money. The most simple first step here is to come to an understanding about the differences and the sources of differences. (Here's a good place to let your own mind do the reference-search in illustrations.)

Henry David Thoreau built his house at Walden Pond for a total cost of twenty-eight dollars and thirteen cents! His comment afterwards was, "I intend to build me a house which will surpass any on the main street in Concord in grandeur and luxury, as soon as it please me as much and will cost me no more than my present one."

But then, Thoreau never married.

Music

While some stress recesses are active - a process of doing something, others are more passive - letting someone else "do the doing". The world of music allows for both (or either) active and passive. In the area of hobbies and recreation, we might surely find the use of music in "recess". The musician (of any level) will say there is great release and quieting in the process of playing any instrument.

"All musical people seem to be happy;
it is to them the engrossing pursuit; almost
the only innocent and unpunished passion."
Sydney Smith (1771-1845) English Divine

I have long admired those who, with or without formal training, can sit down at the piano and create and recreate melody. In these notes, I certainly commend anyone who has any ability to make that a choosing as a recess for joy and respit from the daily chores of life. The great Bard spoke more than once in this accord. I especially enjoy this line:

"Preposterous ass! That never read so far to know the cause why music was ordained! Was it not to refresh the mind of man, after his studies, or from his unusual pain."
William Shakespeare (1564-1616)

In this little essay, however, I will dwell more on the passive side, rather than on the active recess by those more musical. I am aiming more at the place of listening and appreciating. For example, as I began this piece, the background was filled with the music of Strauss. A great deal of my enjoyment of music is that I do not listen as a critic. I don't have to understand it to enjoy it. (Now the whole mood has changed, because the sound is now that of the track from the movie "Medicine Man".) While to the musical expert, these may seem like two antithetical pieces, for me and for this "moment" they are fine and they fulfill two requirements for my present purpose:

I like them . . . and neither one has words.

Words might be distracting. (Remember my

broken hearted friend in the first chapter?) Also some melodies might be too image-bearing. An example of beautiful, but painful music is the soundtrack for "Somewhere In Time".

Background music can be very relaxing; that's why many choose music while in the dental chair. It can sometimes actually be hypontic in its soothing quality. When we're reading or studying, good music in the background helps soak up other distractions, like voices, other electronics. In that way, music can be like a sound barrier. If the mind wanders, it may bounce off the music and back to the task at hand, even if the task is to relax. One may not even be aware of background music until there is a lull, lapse, or plateau in the studying or reading. Actually, listening to the music may, in itself, be quieting. Most of us can identify music that carries this quality.

Other forms of music will carry a kind of intensity. It may, in itself, be distracting or stressful. (Most opera, if the words could be understood, would be stressful. The content is usually about human pain and suffering.) The choice of music, therefore, is a major concern. For those of us that will use music as stress-recess, we should, at least, understand how the music affects us. Not just <u>any</u> music will do. For example, imagine the person with marital conflict trying to relax to music the carries. . .

"Words - at twenty paces, Lord . . .
It's love we're gunnin' down!"
Alabama

or the old

"Torn between two lovers."

Music, chosen well, can, indeed, be powerful:

"There is no feeling, except the extremes
of fear and grief, that does not
find relief in music."
George Eliot . . . (Mary Ann Evans Cross)
(1819-1880) English Novelist

There are probably many who would say that even fear and grief are brought into some comfort by music. While music can distract us from relaxation and peace, it can also distract us from the preoccupation with pain. It can, as well, remind us of more beautiful, soothing moments in time.   Music can bring the smile of gentle memories, as well as the tears of pains past. French writer Balzac (1799-1850) seemed to understand that.   He knew his need for music, especially during depressive periods.   In his biography of Balzac, Andre Maurois writes:

"He (Balzac) had always loved music,
but in Italy he learned how it speaks
to the spirit, evoking the stir of emotions
that cannot be defined and perhaps
have never been experienced.
'Yesterday [Balzac wrote to Eve] I heard
Beethoven's Symphony in C Minor.
Beethoven is the one man who has taught
me to feel jealousy.   I would rather have
been Bethoven than Rossini or Mozart.
There is in him a divine power . . . No,
the writer's gift does not afford any similar
satisfaction, for what we paint is finite
and determined, whereas what Beethoven
flings at you is infinite . . .'"

Prometheus/The Life of Balzac
Andre Maurois

And Beethoven, himself, put the same thing simply:

> *"Music is the mediator between the*
> *spiritual and the sensual life."*
> *Ludwig van Beethoven (1770-1827)*
> *German Composer*

N·N·N·N·N·NO!... Say It!

For any of us, "No" is one of the first and shortest words we'll ever use; for many of us, it's the most difficult. How many times do we say "Yes" or "Okay" purely out of guilt, duty, or constraint? We can load these two words ("Yes" and "No") with so much extra baggage. Some examples:

"If I say 'No', they won't like me."

"If I say 'No', they'll think I don't care."

"If I say 'No', he'll never ask me again."

"If I say 'No', they'll think I'm a 'chicken'."

Naturally, the issue of self-esteem may, again, be connected here. If I <u>need</u> approval for the sake of my personal identity, it may be more difficult to say "No". Some will be most vulnerable here. (Maybe we should say "No" just to see if the world falls apart. Of course, there are times o say "Yes" just for someone else's sake...just to take care of someone else and their feelings...but <u>not all the time!</u>

NO EXCUSE NECESSARY! You don't have

to give an excuse! Some people ask for something and then, if answered "No", automatically ask, "Why not?" Frankly, that may be none of their business. Does that seem rude? Think about it. "I said 'No'...That's enough. No reason or excuse is necessary." Note: This is not a "parenting" book. This is more on a social level; however, I frankly give kids the same freedom. Actually, in the game-playing of life, if you ask me for an excuse, I may have to make one up...just for <u>your</u> sake. (I may have to say something like... "A month from now? Oh, no, I can't...I have a funeral that day." Ludicrous? It may be just as ludicrous to always have to give reasons and excuses to some people.) Again, some of you have no difficulty saying "No"; you might not, however, always be sensitive to those who suffer great difficulty saying that little word. If you don't understand this, then you may, at times, be one of the manipulative abusers who easily disregard personal territorial limits.

The subject of "No"-saying can cover all relationships...dating, sex, church committees, social contacts. Yes, there are limits. It might not be wise to contest the the boss's request for a work assignment; and there are other issues at play in family relationships. But in most of life, saying "no" is an issue of setting personal limits and drawing lines for the other person to understand. I've had more than one occasion to say, "I'm saying 'Yes' to this request <u>only</u> for your sake." Or how about this one: "You're using me; I just want you to know that I know it."

Sometimes "No" is the kindest answer that can be given. ("No, thank you" can be a nice and gentle phrase.)

Think of the dating situation: "If you love me, you'll say 'Yes.'"

"I love you enough to say 'No' and hope that you'll stick around anyway."

Saying "No", it seems to me is sometimes difficult, usually risky, always courageous. If you've rarely been able to say "no", you'll even find it adventuresome.

Organize... Your Way

Order and Organization are cardinal rules for most of us. Ben Franklin, who certainly got a lot done, said, "A place for everything, everything in its place." (You might have thought Mom or Dad invented that one!) In my search, the greatest share of quotes and comments on this subject are ten to one in favor of the real organizers, like Pope: "Order is heaven's first law."

In approaching this subject for Stress Recess, I'll admit, it's too easy to be cynical, even sarcastic, since some might call me "organizationally impaired". While I can have a lot of fun with this issue, it is a tremendously stressful one for many. I hold an admiration for the naturally organized. I do believe some of my organized friends actually enjoy more leisure time than some of you who seem more chaotic. It can, indeed, be stressful if you're always hurrying to catch up or pick up.

Extremes can be found on both sides, however, so that both the ultra-organized and the "organizationally impaired" may find themselves frozen into inactivity. For some, the accomplishment and the goal itself is just organizing. That's great if that person is <u>paid</u> to organize. I'm honestly grateful to have naturally good organizers around. In keeping with saying "No", one basis for me is never to say "yes" to a task which assures a lot of detail and organization. I have neither the skill nor the interest that others might have. Let them do it. They might even enjoy it!

Between the organized and the disorganized...the two can drive each other to complete distraction. Obvious by the quotes, some even make this a moral issue. (It's especially interesting when the two are married! It's probably a good thing to check out the propensity for one or the other before getting "hitched".) People who always have to be on perfect schedule should avoid certain kinds of work...like working with other people and <u>their</u> schedules. The world is not always in total control and in total order. Some of us live easier with that reality. Things may not always be "black or white". Some of us live easier with that ambiguity.

It's probably wise to gain some understanding of your own style of "organization". One secretary filed certain people, regardless of last names, all under "T"...for "Trouble-maker"; others under "N"...for "Never pays bills". She used the same alphabet...but in her own way. Some have chaotic, even messy desks...but they always know where everything is. That's fine...as long as no one else has to know. If this is an area of interest to you, I hope you are moving through your own mind with your favorite examples. This is another territorial issue. My style of organization may seem disorganized to someone else...but if it works for me, that's what matters. Conflicts arise when we cross over into someone else's time and territory. In this world, I believe it really does take all kinds. The obsessively organized and the "organizationally impaired" and all in between may have to adjust and learn at times. Meanwhile, I still sometimes have to hang my sign over my desk that says, "Bless This Mess!"

Prune.... Pace.... Prioritize

Let's throw another triad into the pot. In the world of stressors, one major concern will always, especially for some, be overload and overextension...too many things to do, too many obligations, too many demands, too many relationships...just too much! It's that time of the year when some of us are in a seasonal routine that fits here as an activity-parallel. It's called "Spring Cleaning", a time for getting rid of things and sprucing up the home after a long winter. We get rid of the collected "stuff and junk" of a winter...and of the years. It's a time of heightened "garage sales" and "rummage sales", a time of lightening the burden (maybe making way for new "stuff and junk"). In the world of "things" we may do this in order to "put things into order". A question might be, "How much do we ever do this kind of 'clearing' of activities, relationships and obligations?"

In the Spring, there is another activity many people carry out routinely and ritually. It's called "pruning". An actual definition could help here: "To cut off or cut back parts of for better shape or more fruitful growth." (If you're not familiar with the purpose for "pruning" in the world of plants and trees, take some time to ask someone who does it every year. I think this has great application in the human world of stress.) Many of us, passively, just let our world continue to clutter with activities, relationships, demands that take increased time and energy, smothering out other opportunities for growth and enjoyment. The frustration raised by this continued "passive growth" can be suffocating to the joy of living. Pruning involves cutting out dead branches (dead endeavors) that are simply in the way and of no real value or purpose any more. A basic reality in life is that we humans are limited by Time and Space. We cannot, effectively, be two places at once (except by mechanical duplication and multiplication). For example, thanks to printing, I can put my thoughts out like this in multiplied form; but, as I sit at the computer, time is clearly limited. In the first writing, a telephone call, hunger pangs, even a bird outside the window, can pull me away from the task. (My mind has already floated out to the golf course...but my body cannot be allowed to follow...yet!)

This is all related to Pacing and Prioritizing. As stated last time, I have friends who are much better at their organizing of their world, so that they are able to enjoy, because of better pacing, getting things done and still having fun with life. In order to have "space" for enjoyment, we need to "pace" ourselves. For most of us, because of demands in life, we need to, occasionally, prune out dead and useless or unwanted (maybe toxic) activities, relationships, expectations, demands. In order to prune (like with Spring cleaning and the garage sale), and in order to allow for pacing and spacing, you'll have to Prioritize ....<u>YOUR</u> PRIORITIES.

Quest...Have One

A t first glance, this may seem a strange suggestion as an aid in reducing stress. "Quest" may sound more like a religious issue, or at best a romantic idea. Frankly, I'd agree that it is both religious and romantic. "To dream the impossible dream", sings Don Quixote, the man of La Mancha, "To fight the unbeatable foe." For some, this may involve a life's purpose, a reason to be, the somewhere that I'm going, the impossible possibility, the great dream. To some this may seem only to be poetic nonsense, the dreamer's fantasy world. But those who know the "quest" know the awesome power of the dream that drives them onward, that awakens them at two in the morning with a quickening of interest and energy. (I am writing this portion at 3:00 a.m. I was awakened at 2:00 a.m. by a present quest in life, one of those "possible impossibilities" that could make the world a better world for some people, especially young people in Elk River.)

The quest is usually something bigger than the dreamer and not usually only self-serving. Maybe that's what makes it also religious, something of the realm of service. But what can this have to do with stress? I'd like to briefly remind you of the story of John D. Rockefeller, Sr. His goal, early in life, was to be a millionaire. He achieved that goal by the time he was thirty-three. By fifty-three, he was the richest man on earth and the world's only billionaire. His wealth did not buy health, however; nor did it buy friends, since he had crushed so many people on his road to riches. At fifty-three, he had neither happiness nor peace and suffered alopecia, which one biographer said made him look like a mummy. One writer said of him, "An awful age was in his face. He was the oldest man that I have ever seen." All he could eat was crackers and milk. It was expected that he wouldn't live another year, so the major newspapers already had his obituary on file. This man had amassed more money than any other person on earth. He had achieved his own selfish goal, but he had no "quest". It was then, one night, that he finally realized: "I can't take one thin dime with me into the next world." Like Scrooge reborn, he began to help worthy causes. He established the Rockefeller Foundation, so that some of his money would be directed to areas of need. His money sparked research, eventually saving millions of people all over the world from untimely deaths by malaria, tuberculosis, diphtheria. His contributions aided in the discovery of penicillin. As one biographer wrote, Rockefeller grew from "getting" to "giving". Oh, by the way, he lived to age ninety-eight!

I think passive existing is a stressor in itself. Maybe we all need a quest that keeps us moving and serving and channels our talents and energies into something we recognize as "worth our while". Maybe the quest can be just asking the great question or being in the big search, or the intense study. We can certainly see that in the scientist, the archaeologist, the anthropologist. I am writing this portion the week of Mother's Day. I'd have to say that it can be a "quest" to be a loving, searching, struggling parent. Oh well, so this little quest could go on.

I'll close this chapter with a statement that may be pregnant (in its brevity) with meaning:
"He's not going anywhere,
　　　'cause he's not looking for anything."

"Most people are other people.
　　Their thoughts are
　　　　someone else's opinions,
　　their lives a mimicry,
　　their passions a quotation."

-Oscar Wilde (1856-1900)

Rest...A Necessity,
No Matter How Defined

I asked a little boy once what classes he liked most at school. He answered, "Lunch and recess". While that might seem funny to me, he was deadly serious. He liked to eat, and he liked to have fun. Lunch and recess were the most obvious choices in answer to "What do you like?" Some are happy only when they are working; some may seem content only when "having fun" or relaxing. Maybe part of our own self-evaluation should include a scanning of "When I feel most peaceful and content". To some of us, in the society of sounds, largely mechanical and electronic, silence is strange and even threatening. To many, inactivity (doing nothing) can bring anxiety, even panic. So, of course, they will avoid such quiet times by filling every waking moment with activity and busyness. They may even judge less active people, people who "sit around", as lazy, unproductive. This can cause a lot of strain and strained feelings on the job and between family members at home.

In the arena of stress and stress management, we all (no matter what "type" we are) need Rest-breaks. This is another form of pacing. "All work and no play makes Bob a dull boy." Contrast that with Homer: "Too much rest itself becomes a pain." On both sides, and all along the line of differing personalities, we all need pause from the routine at times. What would music be without rest stops, pauses in process in order to recharge and refresh. No, sleep is not enough! Sleep is one form of rest, and the body demands it. But the psyche needs other forms, even conscious change - rest that shifts and refocuses the mind. For some, that might be actually "doing nothing", to turn off all activity, all thinking. For others, it's making a shift in activity. The hobby wood carver, the stamp collector, the hobby seamstress will all find rest, release, and peace in the quiet of those endeavors. To them, these activities will not be labeled as "work". To the person who has to think, cogitate, analyze for a living, a change in pace is indicated to give the system, including the mind, a rest. Einstein once related that his greatest thoughts came to him while he was shaving.

Yes, it should be mentioned that some probably will have stress problems because they don't do or think enough. "Rest is valuable only in so far as it is a contrast. Pursued as an end, it becomes a most pitiable condition." (-D. Swing)

The chronic pursuit of only leisure might be a sickness in itself. While this might seem a harsh judgment, I will make some observations in that regard in the next chapter.

Now, in keeping with the concept of Stress Recess, I am respecting the containment of the page, which forces me to stop at this point. I will now go to prepare to mow my lawn. My preparation is to sit for a peaceful while and watch it grow...Ah, sweet rest!

Service

Another phase-choice in reducing stress in life is, I believe, to choose to serve, to be of service. Some seem to think that finding happiness is simply serving one's self. (To expand on the "S" in Stress Recess, we might look at what ultimately makes up the "self".) To serve only one's self becomes selfishness, where I see only <u>my</u> needs, <u>my</u> wants, to the exclusion of others and the community beyond <u>my</u> self. This is, of course, connected to "love". If all I have is self-love, ultimately that is all I <u>will</u> have...myself...loneliness, indeed!

Serving could be identified as helping, aiding, or being of use. In the broad scope of life, there is much more than just being "satisfied". I mention the word "satisfaction" because I hear so many say that if they just have what they "want", they'll be satisfied and then happy, and then content. Most of us live long enough (or deeply enough) to learn that "satisfaction" is short-lived and is not meant to be the goal of life. So far, in my own pilgrimage, the "happy" and "content" people I know are invested in a life that seeks to reach beyond the self, to be of use, to aid, to help others. There is also a kind of economy in all of this as well. "Light is the task where many share the toil." (Homer) Service takes us beyond the strictly personal and private; it is a community issue. Being of use in the aid of others takes us beyond ourselves and connects us. For many of us, maybe it is in aiding others that we find ourselves.

In this area, I feel constrained to comment on a concern that is a major stressor to many who already care and give their caring in the community. We are, I believe, burning out many of our care-givers. The societal needs and causes are so numerous and massive that many of those who take on the burden of service are overwhelmed. Not everyone is sensitive to the needs around them; they may not know or feel enough to care. However, the sensitive ones (and there are those who are supersensitive) are sometimes aware and alert to the needs to the degree that they take on more than their share of society's burdens. This problem (at least, I see it as a problem) is intensified by the increased "awareness" due to the expanded mass of information given by media pervasiveness. While this may not be a stressor to everyone, least of all to the insensitive and uncaring in our society, it is a great stressor to the caregivers among us. In these closing lines, let me give a local example. In our community there is a much professed need for services to community youth, probably a need for a youth center. Many see the need, some have gone to great lengths to make some establishment of concrete manifestation. The frustration is in knowing the needs, seeing the possibilities, having the vision, and...yet...not being able to ground it in reality.

Another frustration is having people say they "care", when, in reality, that "caring" doesn't bring any fruit. A way to say this is to quote the Master: "The fields are white to harvest, but laborers are few."

One thing is sure: "The one who serves will always have work." (Erickson)

Territory...Establish Yours

Some of you will remember the pop singer, Johnny Ray. When I was a kid, he was most known for the songs "Little White Cloud That Cried" and "Cry" (obviously both sad). Because he was successful as a singer and made a fortune from the music market, he could live the life of the "rich and famous". While not a fan, I noticed when he dropped off the charts and out of public sight. Years later, when I'd reached my adult life, he resurfaced again in the news: "Johnny Ray spent years and much of his fortune travelling all over the world in search of happiness. He didn't find it. But when he returned to his home area, he found the happiness and faith he'd wandered the world to find." Some of you will understand a facet of what I'm describing here when I mention the moral of <u>The Wizard of Oz</u> or the theme of the little classic, <u>Acres of Diamonds</u>.

If happiness is related to the issue of stress, it may be that it is found in moments of bliss or joy or a sigh of comfort, rather than as a lifetime of peaceful bliss or constant exuberance. For example, we'll sometimes hear the success-motivationalists say, "If you're not thrilled to get up and charge to work every morning, get out of that job!" I, personally, used to get a bit depressed by that statement, because I am not always happy to go to "work". I, for one, do not always love what I do. It is not fun or enjoyable to see people depressed or in marital conflict or children in pain. A shift in thinking and perception helped me years ago when I reached an awareness: "I do not <u>love</u> what I do; I <u>believe</u> in it." It is fun (for me) to give motivational talks (like the success-motivationalist); I am not required to enjoy counseling other people. I might have to be a bit sadistic to be in that mode!

In identifying my "territory" in life, I might be choosing a certain direction my life will take. For some of us, choosing a certain work will determine where we will live. If I were I writer, I could, today, live anywhere in the country, computer-print my work and fax it in to any office or publisher. Amazing, isn't it, what technology does to affect our options in this world? However, as we've seen before, technology also complicates our choices. The telephone and the beeper can make us always reachable and too available at the same time. Therefore, we have to make some "territorial" decisions about how much we want to "cover" in this world and with our lives...and what trade-offs are involved. How much of the market pie do I want to take...and how much do I need? (Greed can be a dangerous issue here...an issue that some never even consider. If you are of a philosophical bent, you could spin this off into many areas, private and public in our day.)

Now, to oversimplify...To "bite off more than we can chew" is a stress-related issue. The generalist, the "jack of all trades" may find it more difficult to limit territory lines than the specialist or the "master of one". I'm a generalist...too broad in scope of interest...and can spread myself too thin. How can I illustrate that?

Maybe by adding and including another "T" as a "bonus" today: "Tranquilizer"...the best one is exercise." (Now if you're a precise, clearly organized thinker...and you can't understand why I just did that...Aren't you glad your "territory" doesn't include having a mind like mine?)

Time

"The greatest loss of time is delay
and expectation, which depend upon the future.
We let go the present,
which we have in our power,
and look forward to that which
depends upon chance,
...and so relinquish a certainty
for an uncertainty.

-Seneca (4 B.C. - 65 A.D.)

Time . . . or Ben, What have you done to me?

Time is, itself, a stressor. While neutral in nature, it runs the same for everyone . . . an hour of mine equals an hour for someone else . . . still sixty minutes. However, time is <u>not</u> the same from person to person, because it holds different value and is seen in different ways. It weighs differently on different people. I'm always strangely envious when I meet people who say they have too much time on their hands, much more than I'm affected by someone who has too much money. In many ways expression about time and money are a lot alike. We spend both; we save them; we can waste either; we can run out of each. But they're also different. The U.S. Government can make more money; some can even counterfeit it. Time, on the other hand, is like lake-front property in Minnesota; it's already limited. While we might be able to "create" and "make" money, it seems we have to "be creative" in dealing with time.

Shakespeare said it simply:

"I wasted time, and now doth time waste me."

or

"The end crowns all; and that old common
arbitrator, time, will one day end it."

While time is, indeed, constant and relentless in its "ticking away", it may help us in stress-issues if we understand how to see it and live it. Listen to the attitude regarding time expressed by the great (and, admittedly, productive) Ben Franklin:

"Dost thou love life?
Then do not squander time,
for that is the stuff life is made of."

and

"Remember that time is money."

Today we hear this statement often. My purpose for quoting Franklin is that I believe he expresses a common philosophy inbred in most of us. While this philosophy can be good and helpful, it is also one which fosters guilt-stress in many of us. Here, again, is that belief expanded to a fuller degree in Franklin:

71

"If time be of all things the most precious,
wasting time must be the greatest
prodigality, since lost time is never
found again; and what we call time
enough always proves little enough.
Let us then up and be doing, and
doing to the purpose; so by
diligence shall we do more
with less perplexity."

While some of the readers will say immediately, "Amen", and "Of course, this is most certainly true!", some will also identify with those I've known who are so driven that they feel guilty every time they sit down or only "rest" by sleeping.

Here's another passage by English poet William Shenstone (1714-1763) which labels "vile" the word "pastime":

"Pastime is a word that should never
be used but in a bad sense; it is vile to
say a thing is agreeable, because it
helps to pass the time away."

To which I would say, "Oh, come on, Bill, lighten up!" While trivial and levitous, my point is that . . . We may live out an over-riding philosophy with our perception of time.

I have already agreed (in Organize) that my more organized friends usually enjoy more production and more freedom than I because it's true that

> *"Sloth makes all things difficult,*
> *but industry all things easy."*
> *(Franklin . . . of course!)*

And for those of you who would show us, even more, the rationale of work, enjoy this statement by the Captain of Industry, Mr. Franklin:

> *"Industry need not wish, and he that lives*
> *upon hopes will die fasting. There are*
> *no gains without pains. He that hath*
> *a trade hath an estate, and he that hath*
> *a calling hath an office of profit an honor;*
> *but then the trade must be worked at,*
> *and the calling followed, or neither*
> *the estate nor the office will enable us to*
> *pay our taxes. If we are industrious,*
> *we shall never starve; for at the*
> *working man's house hunger looks in,*

> *but dares not enter. Nor will*
> *the bailiff or the constable enter,*
> *for industry pays debts, while*
> *idleness and neglect increases them."*

"No pain, no gain" - Did you know Franklin said it back in the 1700's? He said many things, as he <u>did</u> many things. That was part of his "industry". "Leisure", he said, "is a time for doing something useful." That's a good thought; in counseling, I have resorted to convincing every diligent, driven, industrious persons that relaxation is "work". That way, maybe, they'll accept it as part of life and sanity and balance. Maybe, again, balance is what is important:

> *"Leisure for men of business,*
> *and business for men of leisure,*
> *would cure many complaints."*
> *Mrs. Esther Thrale (1741-1821) English*
> *Author*

By Ben's system, even flying a kite had clear and useful purpose. I fly a kite to have fun with my grandchildren. If that's intent and purpose, so be it.

Meanwhile, we'll keep playing with time. I

know a few people who set their watches and car clocks ten minutes ahead, so they'll fool themselves into being "on time". They still seem to run ten minutes late.

I think it is in "Poor Richard's Almanac" that Ben wrote:

"The early bird gets the worm."

Good advice . . .
but I'll bet he never saw a
Minnesota nightcrawler!

Unlimit Yourself

This morning, a peaceful morning, I felt a tight knot in my back, below the right shoulder. As soon as the pain struck, I knew exactly what it was. It was tension from irritation, frustration, anger...directly related to a present situation of stress. I was under <u>time limitation</u> with too many things to do and too little time to do them. I could not eliminate any of the duties or expectation, some of which involved other people. The knot in my shoulder did not start, however, until another stressor came into my awareness. This stressor involved a longtime old nemesis of mine, paperwork and financial (insurance) detail. The details are not important here, except to indicate an apparent mistake made by my insurance company that needed to be clarified. Meanwhile, none of these duties, including this clarification, could be put off until tomorrow. Tomorrow was already shot, consumed by other commitments. I decided to call the company and see if <u>they</u> would straighten out <u>their</u> computer. A very nice young lady began by asking me questions, using a language of three-letter words, most of which I didn't understand...words like IRA, SEP, TRS. Now, I did not want to be stressful to her, so I apologized for my ignorance and the taking of her time. However, I persisted in my pursuit of straightening out the company's error. (Meanwhile, I was aware that she was implying that maybe <u>I</u> had made the mistake!)

Okay...let's break from the narrative and go to the purpose for its use regarding stress. I was a prime candidate for a stress reaction because:

      1. I was under time pressure
      2. With too many commitments
      3. Frustrated, because it was too nice to work anyway

But the knot of pain didn't begin until I started dealing with the insurance issue and the insurance company. While no one else may be affected the same way in this kind of situation, I am, at times, because of an added factor:

      4. I have this <u>limitation</u>...I do not understand "Insurancese". To me all of these

three-letter words...IRA, SEP, TRS, sound like <u>IRS!</u>

Anger and frustration come in with a form of fear. (Surely, by now, more than a few readers might be recognizing something close to home. If you don't understand this, ask someone who is dyslexic.)

Sometimes, the limitations we face may be more debilitating, like panic states that flash back to childhood trauma, anger (even rage) rooted back in old emotional hurts, guilt pains from damage we've done, difficulties in dealing with certain personality-types. <u>Unlimiting</u> ourselves may be carried out by facing some of our issues of limitation, by educating ourselves out of some of the fear, by making better use of people who do understand and can help. While I have used a rather light, personal example here, there are many kinds of limitations hindering many of us in daily life. For my part, I have just ordered an Insurancese Dictionary!

Value Your Uniqueness

To some this would seem obvious, so obvious that the phrase VALUE YOUR UNIQUENESS would seem redundant. However, it is another group of people that I address here...those who do not value themselves _or_ their specialness. Indeed, there are those who, in growing older, lose more and more ground on the grasp of balance and purpose in life...just because they give little or no credit to their own personal and special value. (They are also affected by those who overvalue themselves, overpowering and intimidating the less secure and the less sure.) For openers, read _Webster's_ on "unique": "single, sole; being without a like or equal (unequalled); very rare or uncommon; very unusual." (By the way, to those of you who are grammarians, I _do_ take intentional, unique liberties with punctuation!)

It is sad that so many children do not see their uniqueness, while they are still children. In counselling a child, I sometimes find it important to highlight special interests or abilities. It is possible to spot artistic ability in many children. I've seen the child who manifests special ability, even when she's <u>tracing</u> another picture. The child who does not find a special focus in talent ability, or interest may find it difficult to find a niche in life. I believe it is necessary here to comment on our public system of glorification. Mass media communications will continue to put the spotlight on the <u>successful</u> and the rich and famous because that's where the money is. That's a system that nurtures itself, fans its own flame, and draws many to its light. This will certainly continue, but it is an adoration of the distant stars...it focuses on the uniqueness of others...others far away. In a way, it puts performance and even greatness too far away, even beyond reality. Ask me about greatness, and I'll show it to you right here at home...in Elk River, Minnesota. Ask me about courage and heroism; it's here, specifically here. (<u>My</u> greatest guitarist goes to church with me; I get to hear him, even talk with him, every week. Or, if I like, I can call him at his office in Elk River!) I dwell on this, because I have come to believe, and have built a socio-philosophical fragment on it, that the great and wonderful gift of video and television has prompted some of us to live <u>long-distance</u> <u>lives.</u> This can be like calling, long-distance, for affirmation, identification, verification of our beings...when a local call would be just fine. It's like calling California for any and all friendship, when there's a lonely, potential social companion right next door.

Each of us has our own value inherent in our beings, meant to be nurtured and used in the community of mankind...the local community of mankind. (We will always have the stars in the distance...to admire and to enjoy.) But we also need the local lights burning, showing off their own special hues and sparkles. Each of us is, indeed, different. Some of us will seem to have no sparkle at all, until you catch us in a certain light. A little child might say, "I don't shine much, but if you let me turn just a little...this way...and then, if you'll just smile...I'll brighten your whole world!" And we are, after all, in this world, <u>all</u> little children.

Wake Up The Sleepers

When we think about STRESS we may usually consider active pressures that come at us from the outside...demands, expectations, time deadlines, losses, etc. Sometimes, however, we are subject to stress-reaction because of our own state of being, the way we are. In fact, as indicated in many of these chapters, most of our <u>stress</u> is probably due to how we perceive those outside pressures or events; in other words, it's in the "eye of the beholder". Today, I'd like to use a specific kind of stressor that may not usually be seen as such by most people...and then suggest some remedies.

The situational stressor is BOREDOM. "I'm bored!" says the little boy, who is probably indicating that he expects to be entertained...or that someone else, maybe magically, is going to take away his boredom. "I'm bored!" says the man, also expecting something or someone to change his state of being into a state of interest and excitement. (To that person, child or adult, we may want to say, "You're bored...and you are boring!" partly because it is tedious to hear the complaint.) While boredom can also be a sign of depression, I would rather choose to deal with simple boredom here...the feeling of ennui: weariness and dissatisfaction. It seems to me that boredom tends to dig in (bore in) and set itself as a habit system at times. Lethargy (weariness, indifference) may be a subsequent effect in the process.

So...as a remedy, start waking up a "sleeper". The bored, even lethargic adult, usually has had things to do in previous life moments. These can be things that actually were, at one time, interesting. Of course, one way to wake up the system can be to exercise. To "exert" is an active and effective way to crack the state of physical and intellectual inactivity. It is also, in itself, assertive...counteracting the passive nature of doing nothing, vegetating. Now...let's break the tedium of this chapter a bit by changing the pattern of words:

2. Reawaken an old interest...art, craft, stamp

collecting, sewing, music, carving...

3. Reconnect with an old friend...(Note: a "friend" who was a good influence and sharing companion.)

4. Create a new interest...or an interest that was in you but never cultivated.

5. Get on another side of life and see things from a different view. (Once, with a long-time counseling client, I took <u>his</u> chair...the one he always used. He said, "Man! It's really different from over here, isn't it?" The move revolutionized the whole session.)

The issue here is to <u>do</u> something...not <u>think</u> about it!

A closing story about boredom. Thomas Edison found formal dinners very tedious. Once, the company was so dull he decided to escape to his laboratory at the first chance. His host caught him at the door, though, and said, "It certainly is a delight to see you, Mr. Edison. What are you working on now?"

"My exit," replied Edison.

And here is mine!

X = The Unknown

Surprises...some people hate them! They want to know...always...what's coming, what's going to happen. Some need to be in total control of circumstances and situations, all the time. This can include having the power to orchestrate the complete schedule, sometimes including the schedules of others. Like it or not, no matter how much we may want it or need it, none of us can be "in control" all of the time. The only way that could be possible is if I lived in a sterile bubble of time and space, untouched and unaffected by other people's lives.

Some will also book their days so tightly that there is no room left for surprise or conflicts or decisions. It may be that all of this <u>busyness</u> also keeps them from having to be troubled by thinking or worrying (that thing some do most when they <u>think</u>). By keeping the schedule closed and tight, I can rule out surprises, even <u>good</u> <u>surprises</u> (serendipity experiences)... If I'm that rigid, the only surprises I'll get will be interruptions, intrusions into my plans. Ever go on a trip with someone who was so intense about having to "get there" that he couldn't enjoy "going there"? (As I write this, I'm at the side of a pond full of ducks, young and old. One big mallard just flew off alone, circled once and landed again. Was he going "somewhere", or just having fun taking off and landing, or he is just a maverick mallard, or slightly irregular, or...whoops...there he goes again! My point...Serendipity...Is he having as much fun doing it as I am watching him?)

Maybe that's why children stimulate some of us into wonder an awe. They're smaller, not as sophisticated; they live closer to ground zero, see the more basic things, like flowers and pretty bugs. Adults may need to leave more time open to be distracted and intrigued by little and big surprises in life. To the little child, every day can look more like "starting over", the memory bank isn't as cluttered and jammed with stuff and junk, so each new moment can be a new exploration. Come to think of it (and I just did!) the little mind isn't as filled up with expectations (of others), shoulds and shouldn'ts, contaminated places and things (yet). Every square foot of space (inside and outside) is a potential...<u>SURPRISE!</u>

On our ten acre kingdom near the great city of Nowthen, I will sometimes park myself for a "sit-down" in a different place, so that I have a different vantage and view of my sprawling estate. In one place, in season, I'll be greeted by the beautiful floating scent of lilac; in another, the "chipping-chatter" of two little wrens; in another, the "whirrr" of the hummingbird. In my lifeguard chair, overlooking the South section and Bass Lake, I might spot a deer or a fox, or the passing loon. (Oh, no...we don't have a pool...just a lifeguard chair.) In this little space...so many things to see, to experience...so many potential surprises...so many serendipitous stress recesses!

You...Celebrate That Person!

As we reach the next-to-last letter in the Stress Recess alphabet, I again face the issue of choosing which word to use, out of many options. Today, I'll mention a few Y-words, but focus on "You" and "I"...That way, sometimes, I can talk about "us"...just people. Throughout this book, it is probably obvious that I have a bias in thinking...that the individual is important and unique, and that one's awareness of that importance and value is connected to stress and stress reactions. How I see things will help determine how I react to stressors in life; therefore, one crisis may affect different people in different ways. Much depends upon the person, the makeup of that individual, experiences, upbringing, surroundings, significant other people. As a capsule thought, remember the excellent title of an as-excellent book, "Self Esteem - A Family Affair". Certainly, my sense of self esteem and self worth will have impact on my stress world. I remember a young man, back in the sixties, who was so low in self esteem that every few minutes he had to look in a mirror...just to be sure that he existed!

Now, I'm going to make an intentional shift in pronoun use for the rest of this chapter. I am going to use "I", "me", "myself", etc. instead of "you". In this way, what you read here may be easier to read for yourself; so when I say "I", I'm speaking to and for "us".

I am a sub-total of many things...My Youth has been trained and conditioned, sometimes regardless of my innate leanings. My Yearnings call me from distant dreamy islands, beckoning to me to reach out, to explore, to risk, to hope, to become. But my present world seems to tell me that I am where I am supposed to be...and that I should be satisfied...that this is who I AM. It was in Youth that I had hopes of Becoming...but now I am in Age, and feel like a Might-Have-Been.

Know anybody like that? I do...and sometimes I'm that "anybody"! On the other hand, there are those moments that I truly celebrate life and my own being, regardless of conflicts and stressors. As long as I'm alive, there will always be stress.

One great stress expert defined "stress" as "the normal wear and tear of life". There is going to be stress as long as we are in touch with the world and with life. As I mentioned a few chapters ago, those who choose, or feel called, to serve others in this world will experience more stress...just because of that choice. It is one of the "givens" of the caring fields. It is an occupational hazard, as there are hazards in so many fields of endeavor. So, to go back, I celebrate that I have the opportunity to serve...but I also need to have ways of taking care of myself, of even preserving myself and my own balance, so that I do not simply become "used up", burned out.

I am unique and special and have special gifts to enjoy..even when <u>I'm</u> the only one who knows an appreciates those gifts. (I play my harmonica only for the birds and squirrels under my sugar maple tree! No one else will ever know how great I play! My dog, Dusty, is usually hiding under the deck. He never <u>has</u> appreciated music!)

Now, please, take a recess...and celebrate

YOU...You are worth celebrating!

"Every individual nature has its own beauty.
--In every company, at every fireside,
one is struck with the riches of nature,
when he hears so many tones, all musical,
sees in each person original manners
which have a proper and peculiar charm,
and reads new expressions of face.
--He perceives that nature has laid for each
the foundation of a divine building
if the soul will build thereon."

-Emerson (1803-1882)

Zeal...Do Something With It!

Before trying to discuss the issue of "Zeal", a definition is appropriate: "Eagerness and ardent interest in pursuit of something; passion in pursuit." In this last of the ABCs of STRESS RECESS, finding a Z-word is, of course, a challenge, unless I just bore you into ZZZZZ's...sleep.

Some people are too intent about everything...too zealous all the time. That, in itself, is stress producing to the person, as well as to others around. They may not know how to "lighten up". On the other hand, there are those who never do anything with intentional intensity, who never put themselves into anything whole-heartedly, who never let it all out, who never go all out. This group is the number I wish to address in this little message. I must be clear here - I am not talking about "with zeal" trying to change someone else's mind or change someone else. I am talking about a personal zeal for a personal pursuit. It may be very important...or it

Thanks for letting me invade your world...and

HAPPY RECESSES!

*The Rule of Antithetics mandates
that no public harmonica
performances will be given.
Carnegie, Elk River Theatre,
and Nowthen Symphony Hall,
tempting though they have been,
such concerts are simply
just for the birds.*

may be ticky-tack. My golf game is not very important to anyone except myself. Giving some zeal to it, at times, can be healthy for my balance and my own sanity. Just as an example, when I am on the golf course, I do not think about work, about people-problems. Years ago, I realized that the golf course is one of few places that I do, actually, "get away from it all". Bass fishing is another occasion that supplies the same freedom and peace. I know that golf and fishing are two hobbies that can make the partner into a time-widow, can consume too much of a person's energy (usually a man); however, I have assumed that those guys won't be interested in wasting their time reading a stupid book like this!

Possibly, the main value of this pursuit with passion is the value of putting ourselves into something, allowing interest to be fanned and expanded, sometimes to feel the explosion of the joy of fulfillment, the fulfillment of having <u>done something</u>, of having been <u>interested</u> and <u>engrossed</u>. While again, this may seem so obvious to some, for others life is a constant void and vacuum because they have never invested themselves in anything...they have never intentionally gone <u>all out.</u>

I believe children usually put zeal into things, partly because they start at an "I don't know how to do this" point. It then takes intentionality, concentration, and serious intensity to learn from scratch. Adults will start something with an "I <u>should</u> know how to do this." In my opinion, this is starting out with a handicap of guilt and fear of inadequacy. Both the child and adult have the capability; both may have the desire, the <u>want</u> to do it. But the child starts with more freedom, more openness; the adult with a "drag on his system". By the way, if a child is inhibited, it will usually be because he was trained that way by inhibited or oppressive elders!

So do something with ZEAL; it can help create another fun and comfort world for stress release. By the way, as I sign off, having passed through from A to Z, my harmonica performance has reached concert perfection and it's even great as a STRESS RECESS! (Only the hummingbirds will ever know how great I am!)

OTHER BOOKS BY DEFOREST PRESS
ORDER FORM

QTY.

Anna: Letters From The Attic
  by Sally Anne Dare (1996)   _____ $12.95
Winner of the prestigious
1996 Journal Award by Minnesota
Independent Publishers Association.

Gladly, The Cross-eyed Bear
  by Linda Causton (1996)   *(book only)*   _____ $ 5.00

                    (book and 18 inch bear)   _____ $25.00

Stress Recess: The ABCs
  by Richard DeForest Erickson (1994)   _____ $ 7.95

Stress Recess: The ABCs
  96 minute Audio Cassette Tape   _____ $ 7.95
  by Richard DeForest Erickson (1996)

Torn Pages
  by Ellen Law (1997)   _____ $14.95

Total Cost of Books $ _____

Postage & Handling-add $1.50 per item $ _____

Total Enclosed $ _____

Mail this form with your check payable to R.D. Erickson
DeForest Press
P.O. Box 154 • Elk River, MN 55330